Helping People with a
Learning Disability Explore Relationships

of related interest

Helping People with a Learning Disability Explore Choice
Eve and Neil Jackson
ISBN 1 85302 694 8

Learning Disability in Focus
The Use of Photography in the Care of People with a Learning Disability
Eve and Neil Jackson ISBN 1 85302 693 X

Special Talents, Special Needs
Drama for People with Learning Disabilities
Ian McCurrach and Barbara Darnley
ISBN 1 85302 561 5

People Skills for Young Adults
Márianna Csóti
ISBN 1 85302 716 2

Lifemaps of People with Learning Disabilities
Barry Gray and Geoff Ridden
ISBN 1 85302 690 5

Helping People with a Learning Disability Explore Relationships

Eve and Neil Jackson

Illustrated by Tim Baker

Jessica Kingsley Publishers
London and Philadelphia

The right of Eve and Neil Jackson to be identified as author of this work has been asserted by them in accordance with the Copyright, Designs and Patents Act 1988.

First published in the United Kingdom in 1999 by
Jessica Kingsley Publishers Ltd
116 Pentonville Road
London N1 9JB, England
and
325 Chestnut Street, Philadelphia
PA 19106, USA.
www.jkp.com

Library of Congress Cataloging in Publication Data
A CIP catalog record for this book is available from the Library of Congress

British Library Cataloguing in Publication Data
Jackson, Eve
Helping people with a learning disability explore relationships
1. Learning disabled – social conditions
2. Interpersonal relations
I. Title II. Jackson, Neil III. Baker, Tim
362.3'86

ISBN 1-85302-688-3

Printed and Bound in Great Britain by
Athenaeum Press, Gateshead, Tyne and Wear

Contents

Introduction

This story is about five people who share a house together: John, Terry, Danny, Lucy and Liz.

The house is at 5, Wilton Place, Denham, Chineham SF11 4VO.

They have lived together now for one year. They have learnt how to do lots of things – cooking, cleaning, shopping… and how to enjoy themselves!

They also know much more about making a choice. Choosing how to live is important to them now. They know what they like and what they don't like; what pleases them and what makes them sad. They have learnt a lot about themselves and about each other. They care about each other. They are friends.

Terry

John

Danny

Lucy

Liz

But John, Terry, Danny, Lucy and Liz still need some help. There are things about *relationships* they still need to learn:

'Why does he bully me?'

'Why doesn't my friend like me any more?'

'Why is my friend leaving?'

'Why can't you love me?'

'Why do people have to die?'

Three people will try to help them to answer these questions – Mike, who works for Social Services, and Clare and Mr Stanley, who work for a housing association.

Clare, Mr Stanley and Mike will try to help

But even Mike, Clare and Mr Stanley still get it wrong sometimes.

'We are still learning about relationships,' said Mike. 'We all try to understand the way we behave towards other people, and the way that they behave towards us.'

'Relationships change all the time,' said Clare.

'Sometimes relationships are good and they make us happy,' said Mr Stanley. 'But they can also hurt us and make us sad.'

John, Terry, Danny, Lucy and Liz didn't think that learning about relationships would be easy. They just hoped that it wouldn't hurt too much!

Chapter 1

Are we still friends?

Liz was up early. She was happy. Jenny was coming to visit again. Jenny and Liz are good friends. They used to go to school together.

Lucy doesn't like Jenny visiting.

'Why is she coming again?' asked Lucy. 'She came last week.'

'Because she is my friend,' said Liz.

'*I* am your friend,' said Lucy, 'not her.'

Lucy was jealous.

'But I can see you at any time,' said Liz. 'Jenny can only come on Saturdays.'

'Oh I hate Saturdays!' shouted Lucy. And she left her breakfast and went back up to bed.

'She is going to sulk', said Danny.

'Bad Lucy!' said John. 'Sulk sulk sulk!'

Clare asked Liz if Lucy could join her and Jenny. But Liz said: 'No. Jenny and I don't want anyone else with us today.'

When Jenny arrived, Clare asked: 'What are you going to do today?'

**Jenny and I don't want
anyone else with us today**

'Play music,' Liz said.

'Play with Daisy,' Jenny said.

Jenny loved cats. She liked playing with Daisy. But this morning, when she and Liz looked for Daisy, they couldn't find her. They called her – 'Daisy! Daisy! Puss puss puss!'

Clare helped them: 'Daisy!'

John said: 'I'll find her. Come on Daisy. Dinner!' and he banged her food bowl. But Daisy still didn't come.

'Let's go and play some music,' Liz said to Jenny.

'No. I want Daisy,' said Jenny.

'But she's not here.'

'Then I'll wait,' said Jenny.

'But I want you to hear my new CD,' Liz said crossly.

'Don't want to!' said Jenny. 'I want to find Daisy!'

Liz left Jenny and went upstairs to play her music LOUD!

After a while Clare asked her to turn it down.

'It's making the whole house shake!' said Clare. Then she noticed that Jenny wasn't with Liz.

'I'm not speaking to her,' Liz sulked.

'Oh Liz that's silly. It's childish. Go and find her and make it up,' said Clare.

'I don't want to!' said Liz. 'I don't want to look for the silly cat.'

John and Jenny were still looking for Daisy. John was getting worried. He asked Clare to help.

But Clare told him: 'She'll come back. She's always home by tea-time.'

Tea was late. Daisy could not be found anywhere. John had even made Danny go out and look for her. Jenny had gone home without saying goodbye to Liz.

Lucy had been out shopping. She was still angry with Liz.

'What did you buy?' asked Liz.

'Nothing!' snapped Lucy.

John was too miserable to eat his tea.

Lucy turned to Clare. 'I thought that *Jenny person* was staying to tea.'

'There is no need to say it like that,' said Clare. 'She was very upset when she went home.'

'Huh! Why?' asked Lucy.

'She was really worried about Daisy,' said Clare.

'She wanted Daisy more than me,' Liz said.

'*You* wanted Jenny more than *me*,' said Lucy.

'I've wasted a whole afternoon!' complained Danny.

John wiped a tear from his eye. 'Daisy's lost for ever, I know it. She hates the dark.'

Suddenly, Lucy got up from the table and ran upstairs.

'What's wrong with her?' asked Liz.

Clare shrugged. 'I don't know.'

Lucy had just remembered something. Something bad. She had been jealous of Jenny. And angry with Liz. She had shut Daisy in her bedroom so that they wouldn't find her... and then she had forgotten her.

'Poor, poor Daisy!' cried Lucy. 'You must be hungry.'

'Miaow, miaow!' said Daisy, as she ran downstairs to find her food.

Lucy hadn't thought about how much trouble she might cause. Jenny and Liz were no longer friends. John was upset. Danny was fed up. Jenny had gone home worried. Now she would have to apologise to everyone!

She started with Liz.

'I'm sorry, it's my fault that you and Jenny argued.'

'No,' said Liz, 'it was my fault. I wanted it all my own way.'

'Are we still friends?' asked Lucy.

'Yes, we are,' said Liz. 'But please remember that I can have more than one friend!'

'I know,' said Lucy. 'I have got lots of friends. But I forgot that.'

Danny accepted Lucy's apology. But John didn't. He was still angry. 'I hope Daisy's pooped all over your room!' he said.

'Oh no!' cried Lucy. 'I didn't think about that!'

And everyone laughed as Lucy ran back upstairs to look.

Poor Daisy

Relationship issues: see page 67

Chapter 2

Why does everyone have to die?

'Where is Lucy?' asked Liz. 'Her tea will get cold.'

'Lucy has had some bad news,' said Mike. 'She doesn't want to eat anything.'

'What bad news?' Liz asked.

'Her friend Mrs Cole has died,' Mike answered her. 'Do you remember Lucy telling you that she used to live with Mrs Cole and Miss James?'

'Poor Lucy,' said Liz. 'She always 'phoned Mrs Cole on Sundays.'

'Poor Lucy,' said John.

Mike went upstairs to talk to Lucy. He wanted to comfort her. But Lucy shouted at him: 'It's all your fault! I should have been there to look after her. You made me come here!'

'But Lucy,' Mike said, 'that's not fair. You wanted to come and live here. And you couldn't have stopped Mrs Cole from dying. No-one could have done that.'

Yes I could!

'Yes I could!' shouted Lucy.

'No,' said Mike. He tried to move closer to her, but Lucy moved away. 'You helped Mrs Cole in lots of ways. It's important to remember that.'

But Lucy didn't want to listen. She was angry that her friend had died and she needed to blame someone.

The next day, Clare explained to Lucy about the funeral. 'It's on Thursday,' she said, 'at St Mark's Chapel. Have you ever been to a funeral before?'

'When I was small,' said Lucy, 'my Mum died. I remember lots of flowers and a big box. They said my Mum was inside it. They were lying. She was in Heaven.' Lucy burst into tears. 'Why does everyone die? It's not fair!'

Clare put her arm around Lucy and hugged her. She knew Lucy needed to feel safe to cry.

Clare went with Lucy and Liz to choose some flowers for the funeral.

'Pink roses, please,' said Lucy.

Clare and Lucy were chatting about Mrs Cole, and Clare was asking Lucy all about her. Liz could find nothing to say. Clare even teased her: 'Lost your tongue, Liz?'

Clare put her arm around Lucy and hugged her

Liz was afraid of making Lucy cry. She didn't know what to say. Or what to do. She didn't know about death and that kind of thing. When they got back home, Liz stayed in her room out of the way.

For the next few days, Lucy didn't feel like doing anything. She didn't want to go to the day centre groups. She didn't want to go shopping. She curled up on the sofa and cuddled her old teddy-bear, watching the TV. Whenever Clare came into the room she asked her the same questions over and over: 'When are Danny and Terry coming home?'

'I told you,' Clare said. 'At the weekend.'

'Will you tell them about Mrs Cole?'

'Yes of course I will,' said Clare.

'Has she *really* died, Clare?'

'Yes,' said Clare, 'she's really died.'

Mike asked if he could come to the funeral as well, but Lucy said: 'No, I just want Clare.'

**Lucy curled up on the sofa
and cuddled her old teddy-bear**

She wanted to be with Clare all the time. She
didn't even want Clare to go out shopping.

'Stay here with me,' she begged.

On the day of the funeral, Lucy put on her
best dress and hat. She put a big wad of tissues
in her coat pocket. As they walked to the
chapel Lucy held on to Clare's arm. Clare told

her again what would happen. 'We will sing a hymn first. And then say a prayer…'

But Lucy was worrying about something else. 'Clare, I've had horrible dreams.'

Clare tried to reassure her. 'They will stop soon, I'm sure.'

'But everyone keeps dying. I'm afraid that you will die as well.'

'Most people feel a bit afraid when someone dies,' said Clare. 'I think it must remind us that we can't live in this world forever.'

At the chapel, the vicar said such nice things about Mrs Cole that lots of people cried – even Clare. Lucy handed her some of the tissues.

It wasn't easy to sing. Or to listen. A curtain closed and hid the coffin from sight. Soon it was all over.

Outside, Lucy and Clare stopped to look at all the flowers that people had sent. Afterwards they had tea with Freda, Mrs Cole's sister. Freda gave Lucy some photos.

'I thought you would like these,' said Freda 'to help you remember her.'

When they got home Lucy showed the photos to Liz and John. Liz said that Mrs Cole had a nice face, but John was in a bad mood. He didn't want to look at the photos. He was fed up with Lucy this and Lucy that. He was also missing Danny and Terry.

But when Danny and Terry came home, they wanted to hear all about Mrs Cole and the funeral.

'Oh no, not again!' said John.

As the days and weeks passed, Lucy stopped talking about Mrs Cole's death. The sadness had left her. She was happy again. But then, one day some weeks later, Liz found her in tears again. She was holding the telephone in her hand and crying.

'Oh no – not more bad news,' said Liz.

'No!' Lucy cried. 'It's Sunday, and I was going to 'phone Mrs Cole. I forgot that she was…'

'Oh that must be horrible,' said Liz. She gave Lucy a cuddle. 'We must keep busy on Sundays. We could do something together.'

Then Lucy told her: 'Sometimes I remember it suddenly, and I feel sick. And sometimes it's like a dream and it's not real and it hasn't happened.'

Liz told Lucy that she had been afraid of saying the wrong thing. 'I don't think I can you help much.'

'Yes, you can,' said Lucy. 'You can come to the chapel garden with me and plant some flower seeds.'

'OK!' said Liz. 'We can grow lots of pink flowers for Mrs Cole.'

Lucy smiled. Liz had remembered that Mrs Cole had liked pink.

The following Sunday, Liz went with Lucy to plant the seeds. As Liz dug at the earth, she heard Lucy talking to someone. But when she turned around, there was no-one there. She thought that it was a bit odd.

'Who are you talking to?' she asked.

'To God,' said Lucy. 'I'm asking Him to look after my friend Mrs Cole. And I'm thanking Him for my new friend Liz.'

'Oh,' said Liz. 'Don't you feel silly talking to someone you can't see?'

'No,' Lucy answered. 'I don't have to see Him. I just know He is here. Don't you believe in God and Heaven?'

Liz shrugged. 'I don't know. Sometimes. I don't think about it much.'

Relationship issues: see page 71

Chapter 3

Has anyone ever hit you?

Clare gave Terry a nickname. She called him 'Mouse,' because he is so quiet. He never bangs doors like John. Or plays loud music like Danny. Or asks lots of questions like Liz. Or talks and talks like Lucy.

But, one evening, Mr Stanley thought Terry was being *too* quiet. At dinner, Terry didn't speak to anyone. Mr Stanley was worried. 'Are you feeling ill, Terry?' he asked.

'No,' said Terry.

'Are you missing your mum?' asked Lucy.

'No,' said Terry.

'Have you had a row with your girlfriend?' asked Liz.

'NO!' said Terry. 'And stop asking me questions!'

When Terry came home from work the next day, he was in a bad mood. John didn't ask him any questions, he just said 'hello'. But Terry shouted: 'SHUT UP!' That made John angry. John rocked his chair clack! clack! clack! And he shouted: 'Go away! Go away!'

Later, Mr Stanley went to Terry's room to talk to him. He wanted to know what was upsetting Terry. He didn't usually behave in this way. Mr Stanley thought that maybe he needed some help.

Terry sat with his legs crossed and looked out of the window. He wouldn't answer any questions. But when Mr Stanley talked about the factory where Terry worked, Terry began to bite his fingernails. Mr Stanley knew Terry only did that when he was frightened.

Mr Stanley asked Terry if he could visit the factory. Terry wasn't sure. At first he shook his head. He didn't think anyone could help him. But then he said 'All right'.

When Mr Stanley went to the factory, the first thing he noticed was the noise. It was *very* loud. Everyone was shouting at each other: 'Pick up those boxes!' 'Sweep up that mess!' Even the supervisor was shouting from his office. He called to Mr Stanley: 'Hey! Where are you going?'

Pick up those boxes

Mr Stanley introduced himself. He asked about Terry.

'Does Terry have many friends here?'

'No,' said the supervisor, who had stopped shouting. 'He's too quiet. He even calls himself Mouse.'

'Does he enjoy the work?'

'Well, he's always busy,' said the supervisor. 'The other men see to that. Terry doesn't know how to say no to them. He thinks they're better than him, so he does what he's told.'

Back at home, Mr Stanley told Clare about the factory, and what the supervisor had said to him. 'They do seem to pick on Terry. Some of the men behave like bullies.'

Clare called a house meeting. She hoped that Terry would tell them himself what was making him so unhappy. She wanted to find a way of helping him.

Clare began by asking everyone: 'Has anyone here ever been bullied?'

'What's "bullied"?' asked John.

'It's when someone tells you to do something that you don't want to do, and then threatens you.'

'I've been bullied,' said Danny. 'When I was at school, a boy used to pick on me. He used to say "Give me your sweets. Give me your money". When I said "no", he said "I'll hit you".'

'What did you do?' asked Liz.

'I gave him the sweets and the money,' said Danny.

'Why?' Liz asked.

'Because he was bigger than me. And I was scared.'

'You should have said "Buzz off!"' Lucy told him.

'Yeah!' agreed John. 'Go away, they're my sweets! That's what you should say.'

'But it isn't always easy to tell someone to go away,' said Mr Stanley

'Hit him!' said John. 'Then he would go away.'

'Oh no,' Danny answered. 'He would have hit me back – harder.'

'It's much better to tell someone about it. To find someone to help,' said Clare.

'But it's not easy to tell someone,' Danny said. 'You feel so silly. And you think it will make things worse.'

'And sometimes,' said Mr Stanley, 'people think it's OK to be bullied. They think they deserve it.'

'It *is* OK,' said Terry, speaking up at last.

'Why is it OK?' Mr Stanley asked him.

'Because I'm so slow. And they know more than I do.'

'But no-one should bully anyone else,' said Mr Stanley.

'They all do it at the factory,' said Terry. 'One person says do this. Another person says do that. And they shout at me and show me their fists.'

'Has anyone ever hit you?' Clare asked.

'No… but I don't want to be hit.'

'Does the supervisor tell them to stop?'

'No, he just shouts at everyone,' said Terry.

Liz said: 'I wouldn't do any work if he shouted at *me.*'

'Nor me,' John added.

'I'm pleased that you've told us, Terry,' said Mr Stanley. 'Now we must think of ways of helping you.'

'He could tell his mum,' Lucy suggested.

Terry pulled a face. 'No thank you! She'd make such a fuss!'

Liz said: 'Just tell the men you are too busy.'

'Say "go away",' said John.

Danny thought that it would be a good idea if Terry wasn't such a quiet mouse. 'Show them you are not scared of them,' he told him.

Clare thought that was a very good idea. 'You must remember that you have worked there for a long time. You know as much as them. You should give yourself a pat on the back.'

Terry sat up straight and proud. John patted him on the back: 'Well done!' And they all laughed.

Terry smiled. 'I'm glad I've got friends to talk to. It's not so horrible now I've told you about it. It was making me feel lonely.'

Mr Stanley then said: 'It's not always easy to remember the things you are good at. But it is very important to like yourself.' He thought that Terry should learn how to say 'no' and 'please go away, I'm busy'. 'It's called being assertive,' said Mr Stanley.

Clare said: 'Role-play is a good way to learn.'

'Oh yes!' agreed Lucy. 'It's like acting. I've done it before. I'll be the bully!'

'You're bossy enough already,' said John.

Lucy ignored him. 'Liz can be the person I bully. Danny can be the supervisor. John can be a man working in the factory...'

It's called being assertive

'Yes,' Clare said, 'the others may like to join in. But I do think we'll give them a choice about it, Lucy.'

John sniggered.

Terry was happy that he wasn't the only one who was going to learn. Or the only one who had ever been bullied.

Clare said: 'Learning together will give you more confidence. You will all be more assertive.'

Mr Stanley reminded them that it was nearly time for the meeting to end. So he asked: 'Has anybody got any other ideas to help Terry?'

'Mr Stanley could go and tell the supervisor,' suggested Danny.

'NO!' said Terry. 'That will make it worse!'

'I understand,' said Mr Stanley. 'I won't visit the factory ever again if you don't want me to.'

Then Terry shuffled in his seat and looked down at the floor before speaking. 'I could leave the factory and find another job.'

'Yes, you could,' Mr Stanley agreed. 'It's your choice, Terry. Another possibility is that you could also ask to work in a different part of the factory.'

'I hadn't thought of that,' said Terry.

'But if you stay where you are, practise being assertive and learn to like yourself more, there will be no more Mouse hiding in the factory,' Mr Stanley pointed out.

Terry thought about this for a moment. Then he asked: 'What about at home? Can I be a mouse here?'

'Of course!' Clare said. 'Sometimes we all change our behaviour. It depends on where you are, and who you are with.'

Terry was pleased, but John shouted: 'No!' They all turned to look at him. He was stroking Daisy.

'You can't be a mouse here any more,' John said. 'Daisy will chase you and gobble you up!'

They all laughed.

'John is right,' said Clare. 'No more Mouse. I'll just call you Terry from now on.'

No more Mouse hiding in the factory

Relationship issues: see page 77

Chapter 4

But you do love me, don't you?

Danny was standing in front of the mirror combing his hair. He was getting ready to go to the pub.

'You look smart,' Mike said to him.

'Thanks,' said Danny.

Lucy grinned at him. 'Have you got a girlfriend?'

'Yes!' said Danny, proudly. 'I have!'

'What's her name?' asked Liz.

'Can't tell you,' said Danny.

'*I've* got a girlfriend too!' shouted John.

'What's her name?' asked Liz.

'Can't tell you. It's a secret.'

'There is no need for all these secrets,' said Mike.

'I haven't got a secret,' Liz protested. 'I don't like boyfriends much.'

Danny was standing in front of the mirror

'I had a row with my last boyfriend,' said Lucy. 'He kept touching me and I didn't like it. I told Clare. She told me what to do. When he pulled my skirt up, I told him to shove off.'

'Terry's got a new girlfriend,' Liz said. 'I've seen her. She's pretty. They hold hands and kiss.'

'What is her name?' asked Mike.

'Jane,' said Terry.

'Why don't you bring her home so we can all meet her?' Mike asked.

'No way!' said Terry.

'Go on!' said Mike.

'No!' said Terry.

'Have *you* got a secret, Mike?' asked Liz.

'No. You've already met Julie, my fiancée. We're engaged to be married.'

John nudged Danny and smirked. But Danny said: 'There is nothing wrong with having a girlfriend, John. Or being in love.'

'So why don't you tell us your girlfriend's name, then?' asked Liz.

'I don't want to,' said Danny. He thought that Liz was too nosy. He would be better off at the pub. 'See you all later!' he said. He left quickly before Liz could ask him any more questions.

Danny thought about his girlfriend all the time. He thought that she was beautiful. He liked it when she sat next to him. She was always giving him small gifts. Some days she asked for a hug. She told him all her problems. They shared secrets. Their relationship was special. He often told himself: 'I will die if she ever leaves me.'

Danny had written love letters to her. But he hadn't sent any of them because his writing wasn't very good and he was afraid that she would laugh at them. He had written 'I LOVE YOU' in them. But it was still easier to write it than to say it.

However, Danny had at last made up his mind. Tomorrow he would give her all the letters he had written. Then she would know. Then he would tell everyone her name.

The next day Lucy and Liz teased Danny. 'Is her name Ann? Is her name Sue? Tell us, Danny!'

He had written 'I LOVE YOU'

Clare was on duty. Danny made her a cup of coffee. He knew that Clare liked coffee best.

'I've got something for you,' Clare said to him. 'It's a jazz music tape – I know you like jazz. But don't tell the others.'

Danny looked at the tape. Clare knew him so well. He liked it when they had a secret.

'I'll come and listen to it with you later,' said Clare.

Danny liked it when Clare sat in his room with him. It made him feel extra special.

Later, when Clare was not so busy, she came up to Danny's room. Danny was dressed in his best suit. In his hand were all the love letters he had written.

'Oh Danny, you do look nice – a real handsome fellow!' said Clare. 'Are you going out?'

'No,' said Danny, 'I wanted to look nice for you.'

'Me!' said Clare. 'Why me?'

Danny handed her the letters. 'These are for you,' he said. 'You are my girlfriend.'

Clare opened them one at a time and read them. Each letter started with: 'My darling Clare...' She didn't know what to say. She smiled and then she blushed. She'd had no idea that Danny felt like this.

Danny waited for her to say something. He was worried now. 'But you do love me, don't you?' he asked.

Clare didn't answer. She just looked at him.

'But Clare, you give me presents. You ask me to give you a hug. I have even kissed you.'

Clare was thinking about what Danny was saying. She did like being with him, and she was fond of him. She tried to explain this to Danny.

'I do like you Danny, I really do. But I don't love you. I only work here and we are just friends. I like everyone here: Terry, John, Lucy, Liz. I like you all.'

'But you like *me* more, don't you?' Danny asked her. 'We have secrets. You must love me because I love you.'

'Oh Danny, love is something so special. I don't feel *love* for you, only *like*.'

Danny was nearly in tears. He'd had dreams about Clare loving him.

'I'm so sorry Danny.' Clare moved closer and touched his arm.

Danny pulled away. He was angry. 'Don't ever touch me again!'

'But Danny, I only…'

Danny got up and left the room. His love for Clare was hurting him. It was making him cry. He needed to be alone.

Relationship issues: see page 84

Chapter 5

Why is he leaving?

One morning Danny overheard Mike and Mr Stanley talking.

'I will miss you,' Mike was saying to Mr Stanley.

Mr Stanley laughed. 'You won't miss my cooking!'

Danny was shocked. He had no idea that Mr Stanley was leaving. He hadn't talked to any of them about it. Danny went to tell Terry, Lucy and Liz.

'I've just heard that Mr Stanley's leaving!' he cried.

'Why is he leaving?' asked Liz.

'I don't know,' Danny answered.

'He hasn't been here long,' said Lucy.

'I wonder why they haven't told us,' said Terry.

'They shouldn't keep secrets,' said Lucy.

'We're not important enough,' Liz said. 'That's why.'

'Maybe they will tell us today,' said Danny, thoughtfully. 'We'd better not say anything to John just yet. He really likes Mr Stanley.'

'That's not fair,' Lucy argued. 'John should know…'

'Should know what?' asked John, who had just walked in. They all looked at each other. 'Should know what?' John asked again.

'You'd better tell him,' said Liz.

'Tell me WHAT?' John was getting cross. The others knew that he would be upset at the news. But they had to tell him.

'We think that Mr Stanley is leaving,' Danny told him.

John ran out of the room. He tipped up
every rubbish bin he could find. He slammed
every door in the house. 'It's not fair!' he
shouted. Danny and Terry tried to talk to him,
but he shouted at them: 'Go away! Go away!'
Then he shut himself in his room.

John tipped up every rubbish bin he could find

Danny and Terry cleared up the mess he had left. They didn't want John to get into trouble. They understood why he was upset. John had learnt to trust Mr Stanley. He thought that Mr Stanley would always work there. Mr Stanley had even promised John: 'I'll always be your friend.'

When Mike came in he asked what had happened.

Danny and Terry said: 'Nothing!'

Everyone was very quiet that day. They were all waiting for Mr Stanley to tell them why he was leaving. But he didn't say anything. Later, they sat with John in his room.

'I know why he doesn't tell us,' said Liz. 'It's because he doesn't trust us.'

'Maybe he doesn't like working here any more,' Terry suggested.

'Or maybe he doesn't like *us* any more,' added Lucy, sadly.

'Or he's got a new job,' said Danny.

John blamed himself. 'It's my fault,' he said.

'Maybe Clare and Mike will leave as well,' said Lucy, even more sadly.

'No they won't,' Danny said quickly.

'Lucy, don't say that!' cried Liz.

'Well, you never know…' Lucy said.

They kept on guessing. Not knowing what was happening gave them a horrible feeling.

Later, at dinner, Mr Stanley and Mike began to suspect that something was wrong. It was the quietest meal-time ever. When Mr Stanley asked 'Can you pass me the gravy?' John ignored him.

The next day they were still waiting for Mr Stanley to say something, but the hours passed, and he didn't mention it.

Finally, Danny spoke up. 'We want to talk to you and Mr Stanley,' he said to Mike. 'Can we have a house meeting?'

'Of course,' said Mike. 'When would you like to have it?'

'NOW!' said Danny.

Lucy and Liz smiled at each other. They liked it when Danny made people stop and listen to him. He was quite brave at times.

Mike and Mr Stanley agreed, and soon everyone was sitting down, waiting. Danny started the meeting. He spoke to Mike first.

'I overheard you say that you are going to miss Mr Stanley.' He turned to Mr Stanley. 'You didn't tell us that you are leaving.'

Mike looked across at Mr Stanley. Mr Stanley tried to explain. 'It's my fault. I was going to tell you, but I've been busy. Still, never mind, you know now.'

John looked down at the floor. He wasn't going to cry. He wasn't going to run away. He sat with his arms crossed, rocking his chair. Danny knew how important it was to John. He tried to explain this to Mr Stanley. 'It worried us,' he said. 'John was upset.'

But Mr Stanley laughed. 'Oh come on John, just think – no more lumpy custard till I get back!'

'Get back!' said Lucy. John stopped rocking his chair.

'Yes, I'm coming back. Going away, but returning.'

'Returning?' asked Liz.

'Yes. I'm going back to college, to learn,' said Mr Stanley.

'So you're not *really* leaving?' Danny asked.

'I am leaving, but I'm coming back.'

John was trying to understand it all. 'You're going, but not leaving?'

'Yes John,' said Mr Stanley. 'I'm going away for six months.'

Mike could see that John was still unhappy. 'Clare and I will still be here,' he said. 'And I'll come to the football matches on Saturdays with you, until Mr Stanley comes back.'

'I'll help you write a letter to Mr Stanley,' said Liz.

'We can 'phone him,' said Lucy.

'Do you have to go?' John asked Mr Stanley.

'I do,' Mr Stanley answered. 'I still have things to learn. I can't always be here with you.'

'Maybe *you* can learn some new things while Mr Stanley is away,' suggested Mike.

'I can teach you to play cards!' said Danny.

'I can show you how to cook biscuits,' said Terry.

Mr Stanley said that he would send John lots of photographs. 'Six months isn't long,' said Mr Stanley.

John thought it sounded a long, long time. Months always did.

'When are you going?' asked Danny.

'Next week,' Mr Stanley said.

'Oh! No time!' cried John, and he got up and ran out of the room.

'No time for what?' asked Mr Stanley.

'Oh, it will be one of John's special surprises,' said Liz. 'His way of saying goodbye.'

For Mr Stanley

Soon there was a lot of noise coming from the garden shed. But nobody was allowed in... except Daisy. For some days John was busy, sawing and hammering and painting. 'No time!' said John to himself. 'No time!' He was getting upset, and was afraid that he wouldn't be finished in time. He worked and worked until at last it was ready.

'For you!' John said to Mr Stanley, giving him a parcel.

Mr Stanley opened it. 'A cat!' he said. 'A special wooden cat!'

'It's Daisy,' said John. 'It's to keep your letters in.'

'Thank you,' said Mr Stanley. 'I want you to write me lots of letters, John.'

'I will!' said John. He gave Mr Stanley a big hug. 'I'm going to miss you lots and lots,' said John.

Relationship issues: see page 88

Goodbye!

Questions to ask
yourself and others

- Have you ever been jealous of someone? If so, how did it make you feel?
- Can you do anything to avoid the feelings of jealousy?
- Can you explain the difference between liking and loving?
- Have you ever confused liking with loving? Did it create a problem for you or others?
- What do you understand about rejection?
- How many people do you *like* at the moment and how many people do you really *love*?
- What is your response when people behave in a sexual way towards you?
- We all play many roles in life. Can you say what yours are?
- Sometimes the roles we play come into conflict. Can you say how and why?
- Can you explain what being in love feels like?

- What do you most like/dislike about yourself?
- What can/do you do to make yourself feel special?
- How do you set about making new friends?
- Why do friendships break up and what can you do to avoid this?
- Can you discuss the differences between acquaintances, friends, best friends, paid carers? How do you expect each of them to behave towards you?
- Have you ever been bullied? Can you talk about what happened and how it made you feel?
- Is there anything you or others can do to avoid being picked on or bullied?
- What does death mean to you?
- Has a close friend or relative of yours ever died? If so, how did it affect you/your life?
- What is your biggest fear if someone close to you dies?
- Have you talked to others about your religious/spiritual beliefs or non-beliefs? Can you say what they have meant to you personally?
- Do you know anything about other religions/faiths, besides your own? Could it be important to find out more?

- Have you ever had to 'let go' of things that were important to you? How did you feel and act?
- What does assertive mean? What is its opposite?
- Why do we need to learn to be assertive?

Relationship issues

Chapter 1: Are we still friends?

- Lasting friendships maintained
- Communicating with a friend
- Possessiveness
- Resolving feelings
- Sharing common interests
- Respecting a person as unique
- Communication skills
- Actions affecting others
- Conflict

Suggestions of how friendship issues may be addressed, with examples from the story-line

1. **Lasting friendships** reinforce a sense of history and continuity that is important to people. Be aware that someone may need assistance to maintain contact with his or her friends, and help him or her to **communicate with friends** who live some distance away. It could be important to arrange visits and encourage the exchange of photographs, the learning

of letter-writing skills and be able to use the telephone with confidence.

> Example: Jenny and Liz had maintained their friendship since school days. Being able to visit each other helped: 'Jenny was coming to visit.'

2. Sometimes someone's own insecurity can lead to **possessiveness.** The fear of losing a friend can trigger a *sense of rejection* and *loss of control* in someone. As a defence, he or she may attack angrily, and may be overwhelmed by *feelings of jealousy.* You will need to offer ways of helping this person to *resolve these feelings.* Helping him or her to feel more secure as well as more confident in his or her own abilities may be a starting point.

> Example: Lucy found Liz's friendship threatening: '*I* am your friend... Not her.'

3. An important part of friendship is **sharing**. After the initial *mutual liking* that first establishes a friendship, it is the *sharing of interests* and *intimacies* that maintains it. But sharing – giving and taking – is a skill that may need to be practised. Some people may be familiar with the *positive aspects* of sharing – kind acts, time spent together – but not so familiar with the more *difficult elements* – sharing bad times, coping with a friend's demands – the giving as well as the taking.

> Example: Lucy had to explain to Liz about sharing her time: 'But I can see you at any time... Jenny can only come on Saturdays.'

4. It may be important for people to learn to acknowledge and **respect others, as well as themselves, as being unique individuals,** otherwise differences in opinions, views, likes and dislikes may become areas of *confrontation.* A starting point will be to help someone towards loving him- or herself and being confident as an *individual.*

> Example: Jenny and Liz expressed different likes and it became a point of conflict: 'But I want you to hear my new CD... I want to find Daisy.'

5. Although you need to be wary of interfering when others are interacting – for example, taking over in a dominant way which does not allow people to learn – do be alert for opportunities where you can offer support and advice to enable people to develop or improve their **communication skills**. Try and help them find *the right words* and *the right questions* to ask, *mediate* and *help them to listen* to the other side. Role play, opportunities to act out appropriate scenes, understanding the importance of non-verbal behaviour and learning to be assertive may also be beneficial.

> Example: Clare's comment to Liz was inappropriate and did nothing to help Liz and Jenny resolve their differences: 'Oh Liz, that's silly. It's childish. Go and find her and make it up.'

6. Be aware that when friendships are strained **others may be affected**. In shared accommodation it is easy for everyone to be drawn into disagreements and for loyalties to be put under pressure, further influencing everyone's moods and behaviour. Your role may be to protect other residents by resisting being drawn into any disagreement yourself, and, if necessary, steering them away from the situation. Offer an explanation of the problem if this is appropriate and does not break any confidences.

> Example: Lucy's anger created a problem for everyone: 'Lucy hadn't thought about how much trouble she might cause... Now she would have to apologise to everyone!'

7. When there is **conflict** between friends the anger may be manifested in thoughts of retaliation and ways of being vindictive. Help people work through and *take control of their anger*. Offer *alternative ways of responding*.

> Example: Lucy thought of a way of hurting Liz and Jenny, but this backfired and upset everyone in the house: 'She had been jealous of Jenny. And angry with Liz. So she had shut Daisy in her bedroom...'

Chapter 2: Why does everyone have to die?

- Bereavement process
- Abnormal grief reaction
- Normal grief reaction
- Anger
- Blame
- Self-blame
- Participation
- Resolution
- Sadness expressed
- Behaviour changes
- Fearing the subject of death
- Regression
- History
- Unresolved loss
- Delayed grief
- Believing and not believing
- Coercion
- Imposing views and feelings

Suggestions of how loss issues may be addressed, with examples from the story-line

1. Having some knowledge of the **bereavement process** will enable you to understand, to some degree, what a person may be experiencing. It will also enable you to recognise any **abnormal grief**

reaction such as prolonged sadness, severe mood changes or inappropriate behaviour that is persistent and resistant to change. Coming to terms with death and loss yourself will make it easier for you to discuss the subject openly and honestly.

> Example: Clare was able to support Lucy through her grief: 'Clare explained to Lucy about the funeral'; 'As they walked to the chapel… Clare told her again what would happen'

2. One **normal grief reaction** is **anger**. As a person struggles to *make sense* of what has happened, this anger is often expressed as **blame**. This blame can be directed at God or the person who has just died, for leaving them, or anyone they wish to connect to the loss.

> Example: Lucy blamed Mike: 'It's all your fault! I should have been there to look after her. You made me come here!'

3. Unfortunately, **self-blame** is also often apparent. It will be important to tell or show people that they are not the cause of the death, that it was nothing they did or said which led to it, and that it is not some form of punishment. It is equally important to remind them of the good things that they gave to the person who died, such as happiness and friendship.

> Example: Lucy thought that her presence could have changed things, and Mike tried to convince her that she had played an important role in Mrs Cole's life:

'You helped Mrs Cole in lots of ways. It's important to remember that.'

4. Being involved in preparing for and **participating** in the funeral ritual will assist people in *resolving* their loss. Without this the deceased person may disappear from their lives and there is no **resolution of the loss.**

   Take the time to find out how much a person knows about the process and explain anything that is unfamiliar to him or her.

   > Example: Clare began by asking Lucy if she had ever been to a funeral before. She also made sure that Lucy attended the funeral and involved her in part of the preparation: Clare asked 'Have you ever been to a funeral before?'; 'Clare went with Lucy and Liz to choose some flowers.'

5. Allow people to **express sadness** by helping them to cry without feeling guilty, and, equally, do not expect reactions where there are none being expressed. Remember that if a person is unable to express him- or herself verbally, you will need to observe him or her closely for any **changes in behaviour** that may be an indication of sadness, confusion or apprehension. It is important to give the people time and opportunity to work through their feelings. Try to seek ways of communicating your understanding and ways of offering support.

Example: Lucy felt safe to express her sadness: '[Clare] knew Lucy needed to feel safe to cry.'

6. Be aware that others who may be present may **fear the subject of death**. If they have never suffered personal loss, they too may need to learn about the subject and how to behave appropriately. Some people may even resent the sudden attention another person receives because of a bereavement.

> Example: Liz was unsure of how to behave around Lucy: 'Liz was afraid of making Lucy cry. She didn't know what to say. Or what to do. She didn't know about death and that kind of thing.' John resented the attention that Lucy was receiving: [John] was fed up with Lucy this and Lucy that.'

7. It is not unusual to find that people **regress** in some way as a reaction to their grief. Some comfort may be found in childish impulses and you will need to accept this. People generally do not function well at this time and any major changes and decisions about the future should be delayed until they are coping better.

> Example: Lucy didn't want to do anything and found comfort in just being at home: 'Lucy didn't feel like doing anything… She curled up on the sofa and cuddled her old teddy-bear…'

8. It is important to know people's **histories**. Have they other **unresolved losses?** Has their past been one of change, turmoil and uncertainty? Has this left them feeling more vulnerable than most?

> Example: Clare discovered that Lucy had suffered a loss before, and that because of this she felt threatened: 'When I was small... my Mum died'; 'Why does everyone die?... I'm afraid that you will die as well.'

9. Be imaginative when you are looking for ways of how to help people through their loss. Tune in to where they are and help them to *readjust*. Offer new opportunities and activities as part of re-organising their lives and filling the gap. Photographs can be used as a way of explaining what happened at the funeral service. Photographs are also an excellent way of remembering the deceased and opening up a conversation about him or her, which in turn will help to explore feelings. **Delayed grief** may occur at significant times such as birthdays, anniversary etc. Counselling may need to be offered if grief remains unresolved.

> Example: Freda gave Lucy photographs of Mrs Cole: 'I thought you would like these... to help you remember her.' Liz offered to help divert Lucy's attention away from her loss: 'We must keep busy on Sundays. We could do something together.'

10. Acknowledge people's **beliefs and non-beliefs** and above all avoid **coercion** and the **imposition of your own feelings and views** about death. For some people, a bereavement will be a time of renewing their faith or gaining a new spiritual awareness. Faith may give people the strength and understanding they are seeking at this time. For others, learning about this 'new' concept may add to their stress and confusion at this critical stage and should be avoided.

> Example: Lucy found some comfort that her God would take care of her friends: 'I'm asking Him to look after my friend...'; 'my Mum died... She was in Heaven.'

Chapter 3: Has anyone ever hit you?

- Labelling inappropriately
- Interacting with significant others
- Gaining a self-concept
- Behaviour changes
- Getting depressed
- Communicating through body language and gestures
- Bad behaviour
- Interacting with others
- Undervaluing self
- Being over-compliant
- Not being assertive
- Having options
- Problem-solving
- Getting feedback
- Making choices
- Role-playing
- Having self-confidence
- Being isolated
- Getting things in perspective
- Giving permission to intervene
- Learning and growing
- Empowering
- Avoiding unnecessary contact
- Adapting behaviour

- Life skills
- Provocative victim

Suggestions of how bullying issues may be addressed, with examples from the story line

1. Avoid giving people **false labels,** especially those which imply a negative value. People may be affected by the labels applied by others, especially if given by **someone with whom they are close**. Labels may even contribute towards a person developing a poor **self-concept.**

   > Example: Clare gave Terry a negative label which he then adopted. This was later confirmed by others: The supervisor told Mr Stanley: 'he even calls himself Mouse.'

2. Be aware of any **changes in behaviour** that may be linked to a work situation. If a person finds it difficult to talk about their unhappiness or concern, their pattern of behaviour or mood may alter, and could even result in **depression.** Offer opportunities to discuss work and relationships on a regular basis, and in privacy, to avoid making the person feel awkward or self-conscious, which could, in turn, inhibit honest communication.

   > Example: Mr Stanley noticed the slight alteration in Terry's behaviour. Terry was always quiet: 'Mr Stanley thought Terry was being *too* quiet... Later,

Mr Stanley went to Terry's room to talk to him...
maybe he needed some help.'

3. If someone is unable, or unwilling, to communicate
verbally, it may be necessary to interpret his or her
body language and **gestures**.

> Example: Mr Stanley interpreted Terry's body
> language in an attempt to understand what he was
> thinking and feeling. He concluded that Terry was
> reluctant to talk about his work at the factory: 'Terry
> sat with his legs crossed and looked out of the
> window.' He recognised a gesture made by Terry as
> one he used when he was frightened: 'Terry began to
> bite his fingernails.'

4. It is as well to remember that a person will **imitate
bad behaviour** as well as good behaviour. You may
need to point out what is considered to be acceptable
and not acceptable behaviour, and, of course, be
aware of your own **interaction with others.**

> Example: At the factory the men were noisy. It is
> possible that they were modelling themselves on the
> supervisor: 'Even the supervisor was shouting from
> his office... He just shouts at everyone.'

5. There is often no single cause that provokes a
situation where a person is 'picked on' or bullied. It
will be necessary to find out as much information as
possible before any action can be taken or help can
be offered. A person who **undervalues** him or
herself will often be **over-compliant** with requests

from others. This **lack of assertiveness** may give an impression of weakness and encourage others to respond in a negative manner.

> Example: Terry believed that the other men knew more than he did and accepted their demands without question: 'He thinks they're better than him, so he does what he's told.'

6. If someone appears disturbed or unhappy it is always of value to encourage him or her to talk about it. A group where he or she feels safe may provide the opportunity to discuss **options** and ways of dealing with the problem. Others can be encouraged to share their experiences and participate in the **problem-solving** as well as the **feedback** process. Use even the difficult situations that arise to help people to take greater control of their lives by **making choices.**

> Example: In the story, Clare thought that a house meeting would help: 'Clare called a house meeting.' Danny was able to share his own experience: 'I've been bullied.' Liz offered an idea: 'Just tell the men you are too busy.' Clare gave some positive feedback: 'You know as much as them. You should give yourself a pat on the back.'

7. People may be tempted to bully others because they themselves have been the **victim of bullying**.

> Example: although there was no evidence to suggest that Terry would have tried to bully anyone, he did

vent his anger on John: 'John didn't ask him any question, he just said "hello". But Terry shouted: "SHUT UP!"'

8. Using **role-play** gives people the opportunity to practise being assertive in their interactions with others, in an environment of relative safety. *Positive* **feedback** should be given to reinforce successful interactions, as this will go some way towards helping people to build their **self-confidence**.

> Example: Clare thought that role play would be a suitable way for Terry to learn new skills. Lucy was eager to be involved: 'Role-play is a good way to learn... Oh yes... It's like acting. I've done it before.'

Learning together in a small group will avoid the feelings of **isolation** that someone may otherwise experience. It will also provide other members of the group with the chance to share their own experiences or concerns: it will also prepare them should they be faced with a similar problem. Sharing offers the chance to get an overwhelming problem **into perspective**.

> Example: Terry was pleased that others would be involved: 'Terry was happy that he wasn't the only one who was going to learn. Or the only one who had ever been bullied.' It helped him to put his unhappiness into perspective: 'It's not so horrible now I've told you about it. It was making me feel lonely.'

9. Always try to help people deal with difficult situations, such as being 'picked on' or bullied, in a sensitive way. If intervention is absolutely necessary then **gain permission to intervene** first. Use the situation as an opportunity for a person to **learn** and **grow**, help a person to adapt their behaviour and to feel confident enough to take control. Remember, **empowering** a person who has a learning disability is your goal, not to take over as soon as a problem arises.

> Example: Danny suggested that Mr Stanley could help by speaking to Terry's supervisor, but Terry rejected this idea: 'NO!... That will make it worse.' Mr Stanley acknowledged this: 'I won't visit the factory ever again if you don't want me to.'

10. It may be necessary and appropriate to **avoid contact** with the person or people who are causing the problem, as far as possible.

> Example: Terry considered this as an option: 'I could leave the factory and find another job.' Mr Stanley suggested: 'You could also ask to work in another part of the factory.'

11. There are times when we all **adapt our behaviour** according to the setting. Be aware that some people may need to learn to 'adapt' to enable them to socialise appropriately. Role-play, videos and discussion may all be part of a **life skills** programme

aimed at helping people improve and increase their ability in this area.

> Example: Terry considered what Clare had said about changing his behaviour: 'What about at home?'

12. Always be aware that if someone lacks social skills, and/or is unaware of the need for *personal space* and behaves inappropriately in social situations, there is the chance that he or she may be in danger of becoming what is termed a **'provocative victim'**. A social skills programme tailored to the person's needs may prove helpful.

Chapter 4: But you do love me, don't you?

- Privacy
- Safety
- Privileged position
- Boundaries
- False messages
- Intimacy
- Personal agenda
- Appropriate relationship
- Honesty
- Objective observation
- Social interaction

Suggestions of how 'mixed message' issues may be addressed, with illustrations from the story line

1. Be sensitive to other people's need for **privacy**. Check that your need to be involved is for the right reasons and not just curiosity. Is the time right for your involvement?

   Example: Mike's suggestion to meet Terry's girl-friend may have been for the wrong reason: 'Why don't you bring her home so we can all meet her?'

2. Cultivate a **safe** environment which will enable people to talk about their relationships if they want to. Be supportive and non-judgemental.

Example: Lucy felt safe to tell others about an awkward situation she had experienced: 'He kept touching me and I didn't like it. I told Clare. She told me what to do…'

3. Staff should always be aware of the **privileged position** they hold, and their behaviour should be beyond reproach. The care and interaction offered should be appropriate to each person with whom they are involved. Staff need to work out *acceptable* **boundaries** for their working relationships to help them avoid giving **false messages** which could be misinterpreted.

Example: Clare had singled Danny out for special attention: 'She was always giving him small gifts.'

4. Being **intimate** with someone may lead him or her to believe the relationship is at a deeper level than it really is. Verbal and non-verbal communication, physical contact as well as spoken language, are all open to abuse and carers should always be attentive to this.

Example: Clare had encouraged intimacy: 'You ask me to give you a hug. I have even kissed you.'

5. Be aware of your own **personal agenda** in your dealings with other people. Are you meeting the other person's needs? Or are you *projecting your own needs/desires* to be loved/wanted on to the other person?

Example: Clare needed someone to confide in and had chosen Danny: 'She told him all her problems.'

6. Evaluate your working relationship with other people from time to time. Is the **relationship appropriate** and **honest**? How would they cope if you suddenly had to leave? Are you fostering independence or dependence?

> Example: Clare appeared to be unaware of Danny's deep feelings for her, her importance in his life, or how he was becoming emotionally dependant on her: 'She'd had no idea that Danny felt like this'; 'He'd often told himself: "I will die if she ever leaves me."'

7. It may be useful occasionally to ask another member of staff how they see your relationship with the people with whom you work. An **objective observation** may be helpful if you have been involved in caring for someone for a reasonably long time. Enlisting the help of another person to mediate or counsel if relationships have become confused will, ideally, enable both people to learn from the experience and will help in the re-adjustment of a 'new' relationship.

> Example: Danny decided to reject any further physical contact with Clare: 'Don't ever touch me again!' He would probably benefit later on from being able to talk to someone about his feelings: 'His love was hurting him.'

8. Involve people in discussions and group work where **social interaction** can be improved. Help people to understand and recognise the differences between liking and loving, and how to respond to them.

> Example: Danny was confused when Clare rejected his love: 'But I don't love you. I only work here and we are just friends.'

Chapter 5: Why is he leaving?

- Losing control
- Sharing information
- Being uncertain
- Blaming yourself
- Making false promises
- Shared activities/opportunity to express self
- Respecting others
- Investing in friendships
- Information giving/avoiding confusion
- Being supportive
- Conflicting roles
- Maintaining relationships
- Finding alternative means of communication
- Coming to terms with disappointment
- Making time to adjust
- Preparing for change and goodbye

Suggestions of how 'letting go' issues may be addressed, with illustrations from the story line

1. People soon sense a **loss of control** if *decisions* or *information* which affect their lives are not **shared** with them. This lack of involvement will make them feel unimportant and may damage the **trust** built up between them and their carers, leaving them feeling

uncertain about the relationship as well as their future.

> Example: Danny and his friends were hurt that they had not been informed of Mr Stanley's leaving. John, meanwhile, was so shaken by the news that he immediately blamed himself: "'Maybe Clare and Mike will leave as well," said Lucy… "It's because he doesn't trust us." "It's my fault," said John.'

2. It is important to acknowledge the level of **trust** someone may invest in a relationship. Be honest with yourself and the other person when developing a relationship. Avoid making **false promises** that will leave the other person confused or angry, and remember that your aim is to *foster independence* not dependence.

> Example: Danny knew that John trusted Mr Stanley and that he had made promises to John: 'John had learnt to trust Mr Stanley. He thought that Mr Stanley would always work there. Mr Stanley had even promised John: "I'll always be your friend".'

3. A **shared activity** such as a house meeting, which encourages the use of interpersonal skills, is the ideal forum for people to **express themselves** and make their needs known.

> Example: Danny was familiar and confident enough with the house meetings to use the opportunity to his advantage: 'We want to talk to you… Can we have a house meeting?'; 'Danny started the meeting.'

4. Sharing information which affects peoples' lives indicates the **respect** you have for them. Acknowledging the **investment** some people put on a friendship, and dealing with issues arising in a sensitive way, is an integral part of that respect. Some people may *avoid* or put off talking about a subject such as leaving, because of *upsetting* someone, or to avoid their *own hurt*. Consider seeking help on how best to deal with the situation rather than side-stepping it, so that upset for all concerned can be minimised.

> Example: Although Mr Stanley's departure was unavoidable and, as it turned out, temporary, his flippant response could indicate that he was either unaware of John's feelings for him or that he felt awkward at being faced with the situation: 'I was going to tell you, but I've been busy. Still, never mind, you know now.'

5. Avoid confusion by giving the **appropriate information clearly** and in language that is *understood*. If possible, prepare yourself prior to giving important information in order to reduce confusion.

> Example: Both Liz and John were bewildered by what Mr Stanley was telling them: '"Returning?" asked Liz. "You're going, but not leaving?" John was trying to understand it all.'

6. Remember to offer extra **support** if an individual is likely to experience a sense of loss or needs to 'let

go'. Consider making it a time of 'moving forward' and not one of waiting.

> Example: John was reminded that he had friends to help him and he was also offered support: 'Clare and I will still be here... Maybe *you* can learn some new things while Mr Stanley is away.'

7. Often, people have **conflicting roles,** and this can bring about misunderstanding. Develop a map or chart of positive and negative life events in order to help the person understand changing and conflicting roles.

> Example: John questioned Mr Stanley about his leaving: 'I'm going back to college... I can't always be here with you.'

8. It may be beneficial for a person to keep in touch with someone who will be returning. **Maintaining a relationship** could prove less traumatic than going through a process of re-establishing one, and could also provide some continuity in the person's life. Be aware that he or she may need assistance in initiating and learning **alternative** means of **communication** such as writing letters.

> Example: John's friends were willing to help him keep in contact with Mr Stanley: '"I'll help you write a letter to Mr Stanley," said Liz. "We can 'phone him," said Lucy.'

9. Learning to deal with **disappointment** may prove to be part of someone's development, so be prepared to talk through and share feelings associated with this. People need time to *come to terms* and adjust to this change in their lives. Offer the opportunity to **prepare a goodbye** which will help to mark the occasion for them. Photographs can be used to remember a farewell or party. Allow *anger to be expressed*, and be understanding if people feel fear or resignation, depending on their *history*. Loss may have been a common theme running through some people's lives.

> Example: Mr Stanley gave John very little time to adjust to his leaving, or prepare a goodbye: '"When are you going?" asked Danny. "Next week," Mr Stanley said. "Oh! No time!" cried John, and he got up and ran out of the room.'